Seóirse Bodley, Three Congregational Masses

Seóirse Bodley, Three Congregational Masses

Mass of Peace
Mass of Joy
Mass of Glory [Aifreann na Glóire]

Edited by Lorraine Byrne

Carysfort Press

A Carysfort Press Book in association with Peter Lang
Seóirse Bodley, Three Congregational Masses
Edited by Lorraine Byrne

Published in Ireland in 2005 as a paperback original by
Carysfort Press, 58 Woodfield, Scholarstown Road,
Dublin 16, Ireland
© 2005
ISBN 978-1-78997-097-5

Copyright of the music remains with the composer.

The *Mass of Joy* (1979) and the *Mass of Glory* (1981) were first published by Veritas.
The *Mass of Peace* was first published by the Irish Commission for the Liturgy (1977).

English translation of Kyrie, Gloria in Excelsis, Sanctus and Benedictus, Agnus Dei
© 1970, 1971, 1975 International Consultation on English Texts (ICET).

Excerpts from the English translation of *The Roman Missal*
© 1973, International Committee on English in the Liturgy, Inc. All rights reserved.

Ord an Aifreann © 1969, Institiud Chaitliceach Cumarsaide na hEireann.

Cover Design by Brian O'Connor

Caution: All rights reserved. No part of this book may be printed or reproduced or utilized in any form or by any electronic, mechanical, or other means, now known or hereafter invented including photocopying and recording, or in any information storage or retrieval system without permission in writing from the publishers.

Contents

Biographies — vii
Message from His Excellency Philip McDonagh,
Irish Ambassador to the Holy See — ix

Preface

Ancient Lights and Modern Vision:
Seóirse Bodley's Congregational Masses
Lorraine Byrne — xi

1 | **Mass of Peace** — 1
2 | **Mass of Joy** — 15
3 | **Mass of Glory** [Aifreann na Glóire] — 33

Appendices

Appendix 1 | Seóirse Bodley's Sacred Music — 58

Biographies

Seóirse Bodley was born in Dublin. Studies in Ireland and Germany led to a teaching appointment at the Music Department of University College Dublin, where he was awarded the degree of D.Mus, and of which he is Emeritus Professor.

Influences on his compositions include a range of musical styles from the European avant-garde to Irish traditional music. His works include five symphonies for full orchestra, two chamber symphonies and numerous orchestral, choral, vocal and chamber pieces. The many commissions he has received include his Third Symphony, commissioned for the opening of the National Concert Hall in Dublin, and his Fourth Symphony, commissioned by the Arturo Toscanini Symphony Orchestra of Parma, Italy. In addition to many performances in Ireland, his music has been broadcast and performed in North America, many European countries, Australia and China. Awards include the Arts Council Prize for Composition, a Travelling Studentship of the National University of Ireland, the Macauley Fellowship in Music Composition and the Marten Toonder Award. He is founder-member of Aosdána, Ireland's academy of creative artists.

Lorraine Byrne holds a PhD in German and Music from University College Dublin. In July 2001 she was awarded an IRCHSS Government of Ireland Post-Doctoral Fellowship to pursue full-time research in the Department of Germanic Studies, Trinity College Dublin; in June 2003 she was appointed Post-Doctoral Fellow in the Department of Music, NUI Maynooth; and in July 2004 she was appointed Head of the Department of Music at Mater Dei, a College of Dublin City University.

Publications include: *Schubert's Goethe Settings* (Ashgate, 2003); *Claudine von Villa Bella: Goethe's Singspiel set by Franz Schubert* (Carysfort Press, 2002); *Goethe and Schubert: Across the Divide* (Carysfort Press, 2003); *Goethe: Musical Poet, Musical Catalyst* (Carysfort Press, 2004).

Message from His Excellency Philip McDonagh, Irish Ambassador to the Holy See

I am very pleased and honoured to have been asked to add this word of my own to the publication of Seóirse Bodley's three beautiful settings of the Mass. The decision by Mater Dei to bring Seóirse Bodley's work to a wider audience is both an important cultural event and a contribution to our living Christian tradition.

At midnight Mass in St. Peter's last Christmas, this prayer of the faithful was read in Polish:

> For artists in love with beauty who work for beauty: may they be servants of the truth, always and everywhere worthy of their ideal, so as to give joy to the heart of men and women of our time.

Each prayer of the faithful was related to a verse of St. Luke's Gospel. The prayer for artists, the harbingers of joy, was preceded by the following quotation:

> And suddenly with the angel there was a great throng of the heavenly host, praising God and singing.

And it is easy to see the hand of the Polish Pope, a poet and playwright, in the choice of these images. Such ideas are equally at home in Ireland: Columcille of Iona was the friend and defender of the bards; Columban of Bobbio wrote a Latin *carmen navale* (a boat song); annals record the Normans surprise at finding Irish bishops and abbots accompanying themselves on the harp. In my own lifetime, I have fond memories of one of our school-teachers, Fr. Stephen Redmond, S.J., writing his own musical settings of familiar prayers.

May the present volume enjoy much success and inspire Seóirse Bodley to other fine works 'giving joy to the heart of the men and women of our time'.

February 2005

Ancient Lights and Modern Vision:
Seóirse Bodley's Congregational Masses
Lorraine Byrne

Although liturgical music did not come into being as a musical form for aesthetic purposes, it developed within the Judeo-Christian tradition as a central part of religious worship, and as a means of enhancing that experience. The structures of the liturgical rites, the resources of musical liturgiology and aesthetics, as well as modern theories of symbol and art all point to the ability of music to help participants to realize a more intense and sustained engagement in religious ceremonies. St. Augustine has accurately described how music heightens the meaning of the text 'and that all the affections of our soul in their variety have modes of their own in song and chant by which they are stirred up by an indescribable and secret sympathy'. Sacred music is intimately tied to ritual forms; aesthetically high quality music has the ability to make rituals more powerful and more engaging.

There is a quiet acceptance that music sung in church is an act of worship and not a performance. The Decree on the Liturgy from the Second Vatican Council, the Catechism of the Catholic Church, and numerous papal documents on liturgy, however, give a different view. These documents presume that our liturgical prayer will have an artistic excellence. 'The Church approves of all forms of true art having the needed qualities and admits them to divine worship', says the Council (par. 112). And according to the Catechism, 'Genuine sacred art draws us to adoration, to prayer' (par. 2502). Standards of excellence in the composition and performance of all musical forms in the church's liturgy – congregational, choral, cantorial, diaconal and instrumental – advance the greater good of the church's life in the area of liturgical music. As Mendelssohn believed, all music is sacred and art pays homage to the Divine.

Art and Reality: New Territory

To the extent that many of the styles employed in English-language Catholic worship today are dialects of the same larger musical language (in terms of harmonic vocabulary or rhythmic organization), Seóirse Bodley's Congregational Masses are, in one sense, unusual in that the harmonic vocabulary is informed by the melodic idioms of traditional Irish Music, and there is a subtle awareness of the psychology of certain harmonic progressions. At the same time the composer's cultural reshaping of spiritual expression draws on a rich tradition. In the early liturgies of the church national character was present in the use of Greek and Byzantine musical forms and, as we move into Christianity's third millennium, it is important to bear in mind that all worship is culturally conditioned. In these masses the composer draws on the past while at the same time employing the art and cultural expressions of the present. In this respect Seóirse Bodley has at once continued the liturgical tradition while at the same time reflecting on the new laws and requirements of the liturgy.

There exists a characteristic ethos of Catholic liturgical music, music that elaborates the sacramental mysteries in a manner attentive to the public and transcendent character of religion, rather than in styles of music that are overly personalized. The merit of these masses is that the composer has retained aspects of his personal style while at the same time drawing on the musical memory of the people. There is dialogue between liturgy and its cultural context as new forms and styles grow organically from extant forms. Or to borrow Thomas Merton's words, 'Liturgy is an action in which people express who they are, and who they wish to become.' Two words need to be kept in mind when one first experiences liturgical worship: origin and permanence. Musically Seóirse Bodley's masses fulfil both: they acknowledge the origin of the people and have, in turn, become a truly worthy part of the Irish Church's musical heritage. Despite this national lineage, they are not confined to Irish congregations but can be successfully realized in other cultural contexts.

Unity and Diversity: Three Musical Readings of the Liturgy

The Roman poet Persius believed that worship is a purely mental activity, to be exercised by a strictly psychological 'attention' to a subjective spiritual experience. In these mass settings the composer has interpreted the liturgy in allegorical ways, seeking exactly the right musical expression for each. Through this the mass text has been realized in a variety of musical forms. The tone of the *Mass of Peace* is subjective and serene, the taste for a more joyful ritual is evident in the second setting, while the *Mass of Glory* accentuates the noble character of the ceremony. Allegorical interpretations of liturgy should determine how the rites are perceived and performed, and if additional hymnody is chosen for the processional, recessional, responsorial psalm and eucharistic hymns, it should serve to amplify the three different approaches in these masses.

The Congregational Genre

Against this theory of worship stands a more 'ceremonious' conception of worship, whose foundation principle is that it is not a purely intellectual and affective exercise, but an 'act', an experience in which man participates. In these masses the composer has paid careful attention to the needs and limitations of congregational singing and has realized a very musical setting within the structural confines of the reformed liturgy, with a well-informed sense for how a rite unfolds, and with respect for pastoral needs and sensibilities. Central to all three masses is the idea of a singing congregation as the principal and fundamental musical body. In different ways these masses are conducive to this aim. Each mass is led by a celebrant or cantor or leading group or choir, with simplified accompaniments for musicians of modest capabilities. For a more fully engaged active participation on the part of the assembly, the music should be made available to the congregation. It is also worth the time it takes to have a brief run-through before the mass: that sense of common purpose which arises when the congregation sings with confidence imparts a great deal of energy and power to the performance.

Compositional Challenges posed by the Mass Text

The difficulties of writing a congregational mass are varied. It has to be singable by high and low voice together, which means the congregational part is very limited in its range and has to be very simple in its melodic content. That means there are inherent limitations imposed by the requirements. The danger is that a composer will fulfil these criteria without being able to attain a real musical content. Seóirse Bodley's own solution was to ensure that the melodic lines carried a musical message. In addition he made use of a melodic style derived in part from traditional Irish Music. This enabled him both to fulfil the requirements and at the same time also to connect musically with an Irish congregation in particular, or to a congregation that had some knowledge of Irish musical style.

The 'Our Father' poses certain challenges in relating well to the ritual and textual structure of the mass text: it is difficult to set because the scansion of the text is not poetical and is irregular in metre. The 'Our Father' in the *Mass of Peace* is congregational song, rather than a choral piece, which means that if the congregation is to sing the Lord's Prayer in the *Mass of Peace*, they have to be taught it. A different approach is taken in the *Mass of Joy*. Here the composer has simplified the music as far as possible. The second three phrases (bars 3-8) are variants of the first phrase (A, bars 1-2). 'Give us this day our daily bread' introduces a second phrase (B, bars 9-10), which is immediately repeated. The remaining lines are sung to these alternating phrases: ABABA. A third solution is realized in the *Mass of Glory* where the music is scored without bar lines; the irregular lines of the text are, in part, composed in repeated declamation, making it easier for the congregation to sing, and at the same time making it possible to sing this text in English or Irish.

At the Wellspring: The Mass of Peace
In an article entitled *Liturgie und Kirchenmusik* published in 1986 in *Communio*, Cardinal Ratzinger referred to the incompatibility between popular music and the liturgy of the Church. While a storm of protest ensued, most of it arguing to the contrary, the majority would agree that the life of Christ and of his church is essentially lived out in quiet celebration. The *Mass of Peace* is serene and graceful expression of the text, and it is intended to promote peace in those who sing it. The Irish-style contours which govern its melodic movement act as a musical mantra to this end. It first appears in peaceful descent in the 'Lord have Mercy' (5-4-2-1), and in 'Christ have mercy' (5-8-7-5). The plagal cadence at the end of this movement leads directly into the 'Gloria', where this melodic movement is continued in the refrain, which rises from the root to the fifth answered by 8-7-5. Of the three masses, the *Mass of Peace* is the one which hinges most around particular sets of notes. Much of the music is based around the melodic movement of the opening phrase of the 'Gloria', to which 'Lord God Heavenly King/Almighty God and Father' ('Gloria'); 'Heaven and earth are full of your Glory/Hosanna in the Highest' ('Holy, Holy, Holy'), the Acclamations and the 'Great Amen' are directly related. Similar melodic patterns are audible in the opening phrases of the 'Our Father' which hangs around the root and fifth before rising to the octave, characteristically approaching the flattened 7th from below.

Singing such music calms the mind; it is most important that this work is sung in a medium or soft level throughout and that tempi are quite gentle. Slower tempi can give the assembly space to contemplate and experience the serenity that characterizes this musical celebration of the liturgy. It is perhaps for this reason that this setting is part of the stable repertoire of music familiar to Irish congregations – though the other two settings deserve to be equally well-known. This process need not mean uniformity in musical practice, but rather the promotion of fundamental unity amidst diversity. It opens up the possibility of common diocesan celebrations – such as the performance of sections of the mass at the Pope's visit – and is ecumenically important as a musical bond between various Christian traditions.

Venture to a Different Region: The Mass of Joy
Music does not express a particular and definite joy, glory or mood of peace, but joy, glory, peace of mind themselves, in the abstract, in their essential nature, and therefore without their customary motives. Yet it enables us to grasp and share them fully in this quintessence. Music itself is a source of great joy and the composer's intention is that this quality is expressed in performance. In this mass some of the tempi are quite fast,

particularly in the 'Gloria' and 'Holy, Holy, Holy', where optional hand bells heighten this mood. The addition of three trumpets in the 'Gospel Acclamation' answered by two optional trumpet parts in the 'Holy, Holy, Holy' intensifies this joyous celebration. The setting is simple but somewhat more demanding than the *Mass of Peace* because it has to be sung more quickly. However, much of the music is sung by a leading group, with additional possibilities for vocal or instrumental descants. In contrast to the *Mass of Peace*, there is one version of the 'Gloria', where the congregation participates only in the chorus. In this setting the close adaptation of the melody to the sacred text, and the strong vocal line accompanying and enhancing the words, interpret their efficacy and force. This is achieved by the use of musical modes that are simple and plain, through the simplicity of melodic and structural forms, from which its other note, universality, is derived.

The Voice of Exaltation: Mass of Glory

The *Mass of Glory* is a mass of more ceremonial splendour. Of the three masses the *Mass of Glory* is the one with the most performance possibilities. The singing can be led by either a solo voice or SSA Choir or trio, or by full mixed-voice choir (SATB). The accompaniment can be readily adapted for a string ensemble. Some vocal descants are also included in the 'Gospel Acclamation', and the 'Gloria' uses three different congregational refrains. In exploring these possibilities the voice of the choir and that of the congregation properly exist in a dynamic relationship; there is no intrinsic conflict between the two. In this mass, a careful balance between the choir and congregation is fostered. As part of the assembly, the choir at times leads congregational singing; at times it simply joins with the congregation; it sings to allow the ritual to unfold more expressively. The choir then has a twofold purpose in this mass. Its primary role is to lead congregational singing, yet the choir also makes musical offerings for, and on behalf of, the congregation. Active participation on the part of the people is possible through actual singing and engaged listening in realizing their performance. Such participation of the choir is crucial to the realization of solemnity and majesty in liturgical performance.

In the *Mass of Glory* the musical content is influenced by traditional Irish idioms. As in the *Mass of Peace* this is evident in the opening movement, the 'Lord have Mercy', which moves between tonic and dominant. The limited range of such melodic movement, commonly found in Irish airs, is readily traced throughout the mass. One example is evident in the 'Gloria', where the first refrain rises from the tonic to the mediant, before falling on its characteristic descent: 8-7-5-4-5. Another example is the 5-4-5 figure of the 'Lamb of God', and in the prayer, 'Have mercy on us', both of which hang around the fifth. Similarly the downfall 8-7-5 and approach back to the dominant for 'You take away the sins of the world' and the final descent 5-4-2-1 are typical of Irish traditional descending melodic motifs.

Liturgically, the 'Gloria' is the song of the angels heralding Christ's birth, and the choir serves in a particular way to give voice to the glory. The additional SSA choir serves to emphasize this approach to the mass, as does the use of bells rung at the end of the 'Gloria'. To a degree the theme of Glory is reflected in the harmonic content, and in particular in the division of the choral harmony into six parts. In the opening refrain two trio groupings, SSA and TBB, run in contrary motion in quavers. This particular style of harmony is concerned with the directional movement of the melodic lines. While the use of the flattened 7th is an obvious characteristic derived from traditional Irish music, the composer uses this trait creatively. In the opening chorus of the 'Gloria' there is no flattened 7th and throughout the mass all of the harmonic movement is, in fact, subtly influenced by Irish melodic style. An example of this is found in the 'Gloria' where 'You alone are the Holy One' is harmonized in B flat with a flattened 7th. Bodley then uses a perfect cadence to switch into an E flat version of this mode for 'You alone are the Lord'. Both are Ionian modes with a flattened 7th. The music does not modulate but switches between the two and adds further variety by shifting to the flattened 7th of E flat to mark a musical and textual apex on 'Jesus Christ'.

In this setting Bodley has created a setting suitable for either the English or Irish liturgy. To make this possible the composer has adopted the procedure where bars are sometimes repeated to accommodate the Irish text. 'Lord Jesus Christ'/A Thiarna Dia, a Rí na bhflaitheas,' (bars 17-19) is an example of this. In particular in the 'Gloria' but also in other movements, the composer has used the idea of a single chord with declamation according to the speech rhythms of the Irish or English texts, which are unequal in the number of syllables.

Realizing the Score: Musical Expression and Performance Practice

In these masses Seóirse Bodley has produced first-rate music for the liturgy: the creation of which is a demanding task, especially if artistic integrity is to nourish both heart and mind when the musical resources are strictly limited and widely varying. Each of these masses is formed by the structure and spirit of the liturgy, while at the same time being attentive to artistic values. The music of these masses is technically, aesthetically and expressively good. Their various performance possibilities make these masses a very rich resource with music which is 'accessible', and the frame of mind in which these masses are approached is central to a musical performance.

One of the clear purposes for liturgical music is that it be a source for leading the community in music. A good leader – cantor or choir or leading group or organist – is central in encouraging people to sing and it is important to give the congregation a secure lead. The major components of this are rhythm and tempo. All of the music needs to be sung with impetus and a sense of forward movement in the phrasing. To a large extent the congregation repeats musical ideas which the cantor or choir or leading group have just sung. Therefore it is important that the cantor, choir or leading group present the music with a forward movement in the phrasing since the congregation are most likely to pick up the approach presented to them for imitation. Similarly, the climaxes in the masses should not be considered in terms of length or dynamics. In writing the music the composer has endeavoured to emphasize such liturgical highpoints as the 'Great Amen'. The climaxes should, therefore, be sung, not only in terms of dynamics but also in terms of expression, an example of which is the final petition in the 'Lamb of God': 'Grant us Peace. Musical judgment should be a central part of liturgical celebration and although the masses are simple in style, the liturgical community should sing them with musical sensitivity. To attain this end it is important to rehearse the congregational parts – this can be done briefly before mass - musical explanations can be very helpful. Saint Paul said, 'I will sing with the heart, but with the understanding also': the more people know about what is being presented, the more wholeheartedly they participate. Each of the masses expresses a certain musical attitude towards the text. Choirs leading the singing should cultivate a style of performance of each of the masses in keeping with its proper character so that the dignity and effectiveness of these liturgical mass settings is carefully realized.

Seóirse Bodley: Mass of Peace

Georges Rouault, *Apparition in the Tomb* (1939)
(Woodcut. Detail)
Paris, Musée National d'Art Moderne, Centre Georges Pompidou

Mass of Peace

Performance

The title reflects the intention that this Mass might help to promote peace and serenity in those who sing it. Consequently, it should be sung at a medium or soft level throughout.

The speeds can best be judged in relation to the Alleluia. This is to be sung at a slow pace, yet with sufficient movement to be comfortable for the congregation. The sections marked Andante are rather faster. The 'Gloria' (Andantino) is faster again – it should move with a comfortable easy flow.

Two versions of the 'Gloria' are provided. The first is to be sung throughout by all present. In the second (the Alternative Version), the congregation joins in the refrain and 'Amen' only. The Alternative Version is thus a means by which the congregation could become familiar with the music of the entire 'Gloria' before they attempt to sing the 'Gloria' straight through, without the use of the refrain.

The 'Alleluia' and 'Great Amen' are sung to the same music in this Mass, and in each case are marked to be sung 'slowly, with the utmost serenity'. This indication should be carefully observed, in order to mark them as points of especial importance in the liturgical structure of the Mass.

Seóirse Bodley

Note for choir and organist: In the alternative version of the Gloria that follows, the congregation sings only the refrain and the amen. The choir sings the rest of the music. The refrain, which consists of the first four bars of the Gloria, is sung by all with organ accompaniment, at each point marked 𝄋 in the music.

Gloria
(Alternative version)

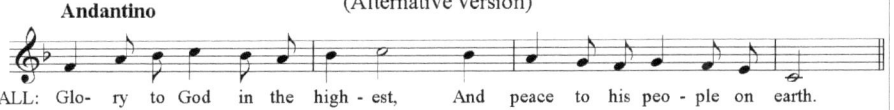

ALL: Glo-ry to God in the high-est, And peace to his peo-ple on earth.

CHOIR: Lord God, heavenly King,
Almighty God and Father.
We worship you, we give you thanks,
We praise your for your glory.

ALL: Glory to God in the Highest,
And peace to His people on earth.

CHOIR: Lord Jesus Christ, Only Son of the Father,
Lord God, Lamb of God,
You take away the sin of the world; have mercy on us;

ALL: Glory to God in the Highest,
And peace to His people on earth.

CHOIR: You are seated on the right hand of the Father; receive our prayer.

ALL: Glory to God in the Highest,
And peace to His people on earth.

CHOIR: For you alone are the Holy one,
You alone are the Lord,
You alone are the Most High, Jesus Christ,
With the Holy Spirit in the glory of God the Father.

ALL: A - men.

Gospel Acclamation

Holy, Holy, Holy

Our Father

Glory to God
(Alternative version)

ALL: Glo-ry to God in the high-est, and peace to His peo-ple on earth.

CHOIR: Lord God, heavenly King,
Almighty God and Father,
we worship you, we give you thanks,
we praise you for your glory.

ALL: Glory to God in the highest,
and peace to His people on earth.

CHOIR: Lord Jesus Christ, only Son of the Father,
Lord God, Lamb of God,
You take away the sin of the world:
have mercy on us.

ALL: Glory to God in the highest,
and peace to His people on earth.

CHOIR: You are seated at the right hand of the Father:
receive our prayer.

ALL: Glory to God in the highest,
and peace to His people on earth.

CHOIR: For you alone are the Holy One,
You alone are the Lord,
You alone are the Most High,
Jesus Christ,
with the Holy Spirit,
in the glory. of God the Father.

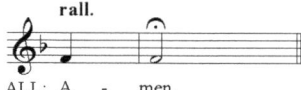

ALL: A - men.

Gospel Acclamation

The 'Alleluia' below is sung by the Cantor and repeated by all.
The cantor then sings the verse of the Gospel Acclamation.
All repeat the 'Alleluia.'

Slowly, with the utmost serenity

Al - le - lu - ia, Al - le - lu - ia, Al - le - lu - ia.

Seóirse Bodley: Mass of Joy

Georges Rouault, *Magnificat* (1939)
(Woodcut Detail)
Paris, Musée National d'Art Moderne, Centre Georges Pompidou

Mass of Joy

This Mass was commissioned by the Brothers of St John of God in honour of their founder and patron on the occasion of the centenary of their Irish foundation.

Performance
Much of this Mass is designed to be sung by a leading group, with all present participating in the refrain. The leading-group (usually designated L.G. in the score) need not necessarily be a choir. Any group of voices capable of singing all the music may fulfil this function. It is hoped that where congregations have thoroughly familiarized themselves with all of the music, particular sections of the congregation (designated perhaps merely by their location in the church) might assume this role. Different areas of the church might even lead different sections of the Mass.

Transpositions
The pitch of the melodies is arranged to suit a mixed adult congregation. For school Masses it may be desirable to transpose some of the numbers to a higher key.

Descants
These are optional. They may be performed vocally (vocalized) or instrumentally, as suitable. The phrasing should be adjusted to suit each case. In some cases suggested instrumentation is given. These may be modified where necessary.

Seóirse Bodley

Gospel Acclamation

*Optional parts. Use only to accompany the repeat by all.

Holy, Holy, Holy

* Use with refrain throughout. Hand-bells or similar instruments.
The use of two trumpets is also possible.
One plays the descant, the other the refrain.

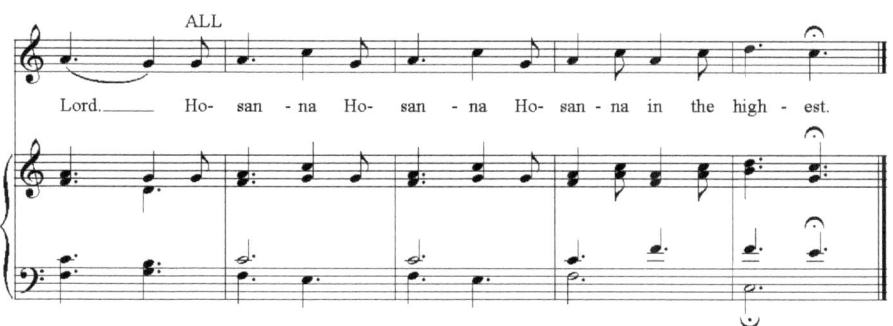

*Each section of the music is sung by the Leading Group and repeated by all.

Our Father

*N.B. This is moderato in 2 (not in 4) - but not too fast.

Lamb of God

*The time signature varies betwen 2/4 and 3/4.

Holy, Holy, Holy

Acclamation

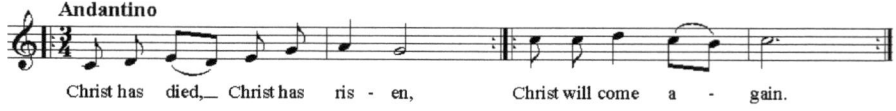

Great Amen

Mass of Glory
Aifreann na Glóire

This Mass was commissioned by the Sisters of Loreto for performance on the feast of the Assumption of the Blessed Virgin, 1980, to celebrate the closing of their chapter.

Performance
There are quite a few performance options in this Mass. The singing can be led by SSA choir (or trio) or by full mixed-voice choir (SATB). It is also possible, where necessary, to perform the Mass by having a solo voice (or voices) sing the top part of the choir harmony only. The soloist or group can thus take the place of a choir.

Texts
The Mass may be sung to the Irish or English text. In each case the words should flow easily and be enunciated with care and accuracy. (Attention is especially needed in rendering the diphthongs in Irish. Where the diphthong is sung mainly on the first of its vowels, the second of the two vowels should appear at the extreme end of a single note or at the end of the last note of a group of notes.) A slight *rubato* can occasionally be used where the clear pronunciation of the words may call for it. The *parlando* sections (notated: ‖◯‖) should move fairly briskly.

Accompaniment
This is basically for organ or harmonium, but could be adapted quite easily for string orchestra or other ensembles.

Seóirse Bodley

Seóirse Bodley: Mass of Glory
[Aifreann na Glóire]

Georges Rouault, *Christ* ((1939)
(Woodcut, Detail)
Paris, Musée National d'Art Moderne, Centre Georges Pompidou

Mass of Glory

Aifreann na Glóire

Lord, have mercy

A Thiarna, déan trócaire

Each invocation is sung by the celebrant or cantor and repeated by all.

Seóirse Bodley

*The organ part also serves as the basis for a four-part (SATB) setting.

Music © 1980 Seoirse Bodley

Gloria

An Ghlóir

The refrain is sung in unison by the choir and answered by the congregation.

*The choral harmony, which may be either SSA or full choir should be sung to the repeat of the refrain by the congregation. It can be used on all subsequent appearances of this refrain.

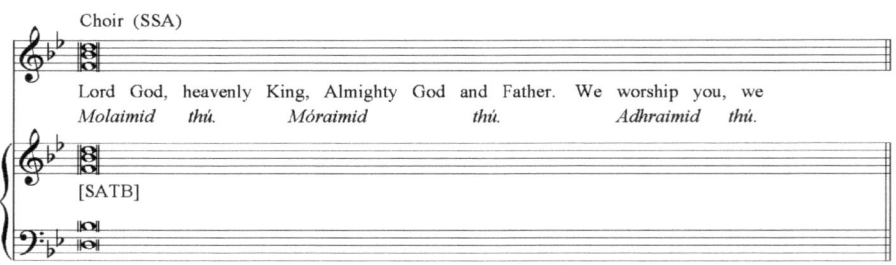
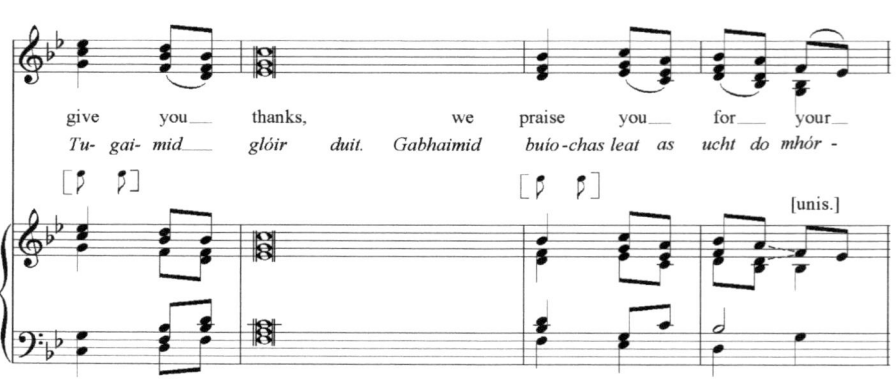

*These repeats to be used only with the Irish text.

*This chord is played in all versions, but not sung.

*The choral harmony, which may be either SSA or full choir, should be sung to the repeat of the refrain by the congregation. It can be used on the subsequent appearance of this refrain (2).

†Bells may be rung or played with the repeat only. Smaller types of bell are intended: sleighbells or other groups of small bells could be used. Altar-bells of the type that are rung as a group would be suitable.

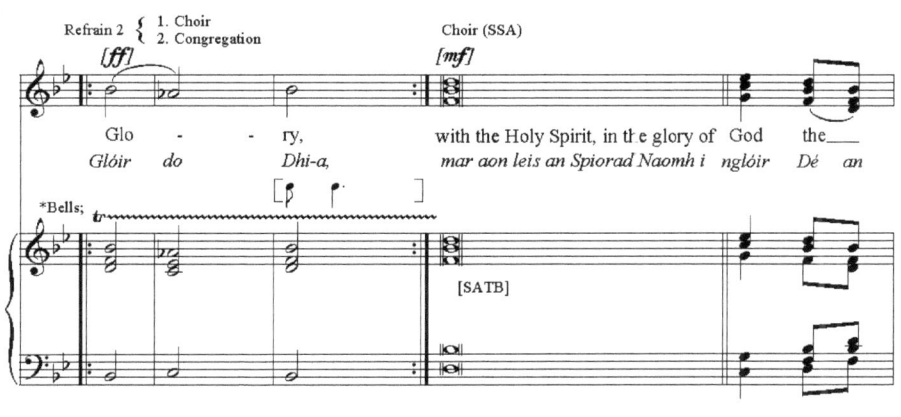

* Used with repeat. (optional).

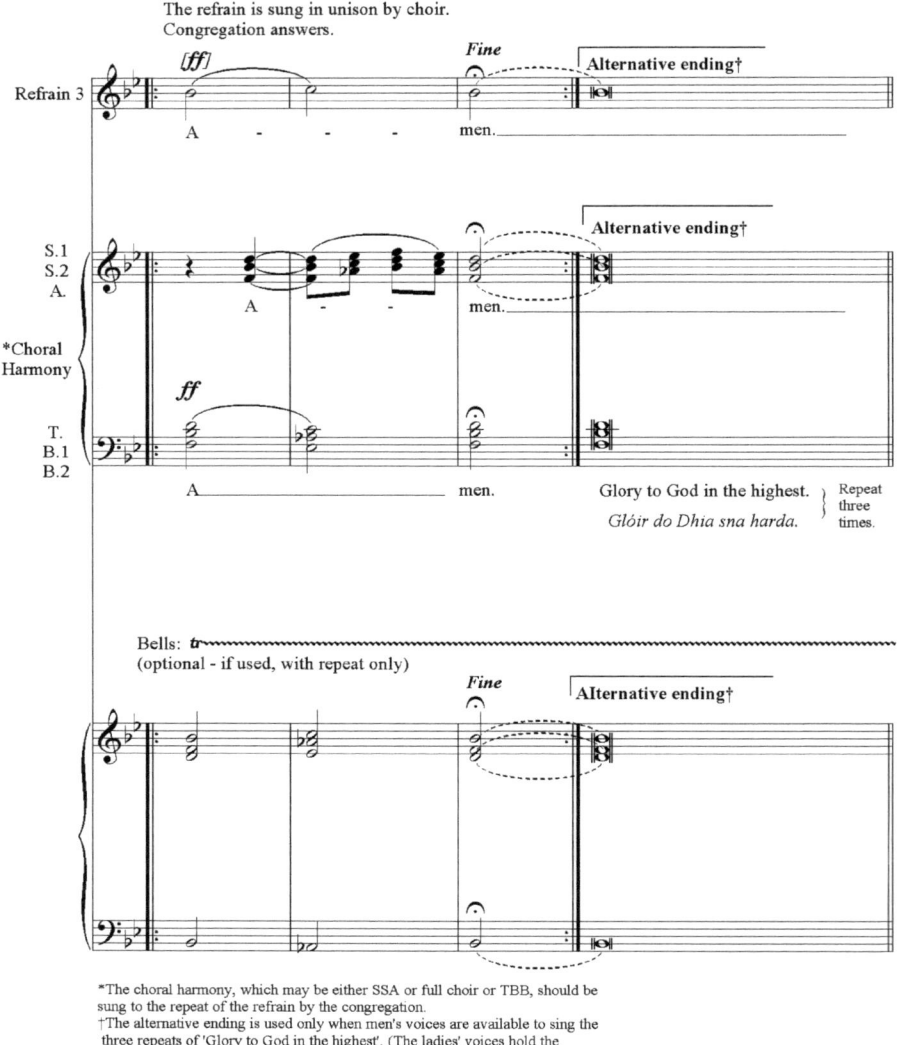

Gospel Acclamation

Ceiliúradh an tSoiscéil

Each section is sung by the choir (unison is an option) and repeated by the congregation.

*In the case of performance by SSA, all soprano voices sing the descant against the repeat of the refrains by altos and congregation. In the SATB version the descant could be sung by a solo soprano or mezzo-soprano.

Holy, Holy, Holy
Is naofa, naofa, naofa

*SSA all parts in unison except where three-part harmony is indicated.

**Choir (SSA) uses three-part harmony for both first statement and repeat.

*Choir (SSA) uses three-part harmony for both first statement and repeat.
†This chord is played but not sung in the English version.

Memorial Acclamation

Comhgháir tar éis na Choisreacain

Each section of the music is sung by the choir and repeated by all.

*For the acclamations in Irish, the first two sections of the music need to be sung twice to fit the words. This applies to both choir and congregation.

Great Amen

An tAmen Mór

*The choral harmony is sung by the choir against the repeat of the music by the congregation.
†The lower stave of the organ part could be used to add TBB to the SSA to form a full choir.

Our Father

Ár nAthair

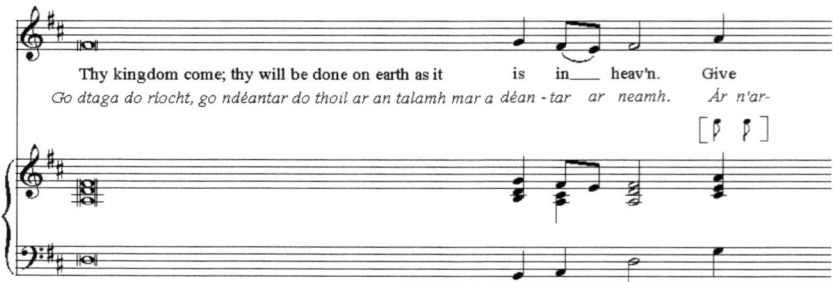

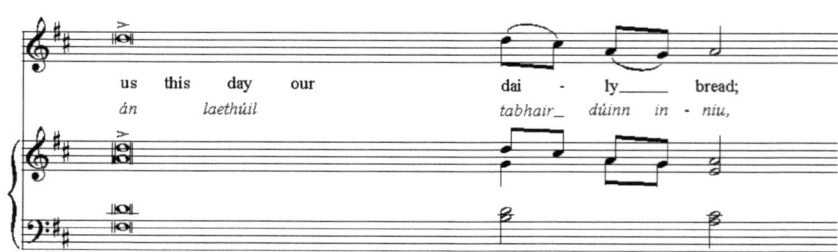

*The passages with time-values should be rendered Andante, otherwise the rhythm is that of speech.

†A four-part version (SATB) can be made from the four parts of the accompaniment.

Lamb of God

A Uain Dé

*The choir (SSA) uses three-part harmony for both the first statement and the repeat.
** The two lower parts of the keyboard part could also serve as T and B to the SSA parts, should a full-choir version be needed.
†The entire first section is sung again, complete with all answers by the congregation, as before.

Mass of Glory

Aifreann na Glóire

Congregational part

Lord, have mercy

A Thiarna, déan trócaire

Music: Seóirse Bodley

Each invocation is sung by the celebrant or cantor and repeated by all.

Gloria

An Ghlóir

The refrain is sung in unison by the choir and answered by the congregation.

Refrain 1

CHOIR:

and peace to his people on earth.
agus ar talamh siocháin do lucht a pháirte.

Music © 1980 Seoirse Bodley

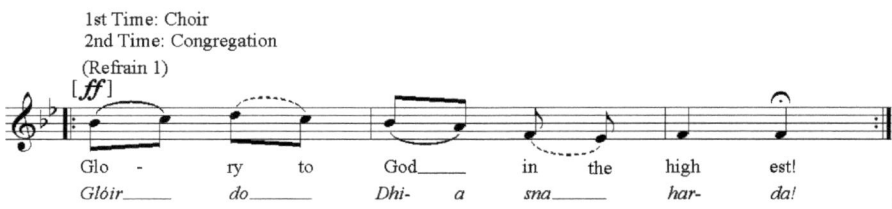

1st Time: Choir
2nd Time: Congregation
(Refrain 1)
[*ff*]

Glo - ry to God____ in the high - est!
Glóir____ do____ Dhi- a sna____ har- da!

CHOIR:

Lord, God, heavenly King, almighty God and Father,
we worship you,
we give you thanks,
we praise you for your glory.

Molaimid thú, móraimid thú, adhraimid thú.
Tugaimid glóir duit.
Gabhaimíd buíochas leat as ucht do mhór-ghlóire.

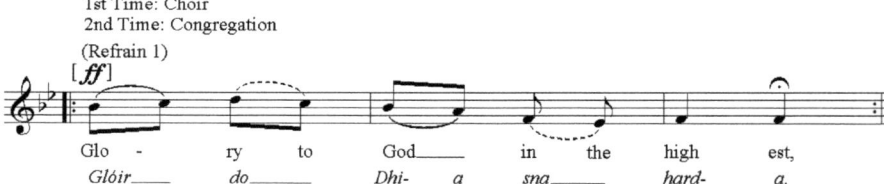

1st Time: Choir
2nd Time: Congregation
(Refrain 1)
[*ff*]

Glo - ry to God____ in the high - est,
Glóir____ do____ Dhi- a sna____ hard- a,

CHOIR:

Lord Jesus Christ, only Son of the Father,
Lord God, Lamb of God,
you take away the sin of the world:
have mercy on us;

A Thiarna Dia, a Rí na bhflaitheas,
a Dhia, a Athair uilechumhachtaigh,
a Thiarna, a Aon-Mhic, a Íosa Críost,
a Thiarna Dia, a Uain Dé, Mac an Athar.
Tusa a thógann peacaí an domhain, déan trócaire orainn.
Tusa a thógann peacaí an domhain, glac lenár nguí.

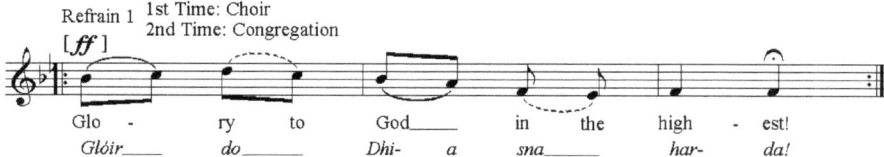

CHOIR:
you are seated at the right hand of the Father:
receive our prayer.

*Tusa atá i do shuí ar dheis an Athar,
déan trócaire orainn.*

CHOIR:
For you alone are the Holy One,
Óir is tú amháin is naofa.

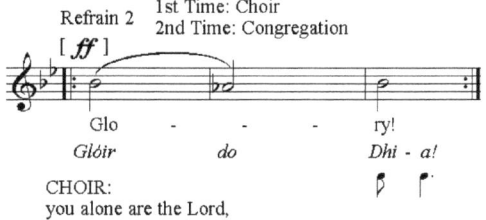

CHOIR:
you alone are the Lord,
you alone are the Most High, Jesus Christ,

*Is tú amháin is Tiarna.
Is tú amháin is ró-ard, a Íosa Críost,*

CHOIR: with the Holy Spirit
in the glory of God the Father.

*mar aon leis an Spiorad Naomh
i nglór Dé an tAthair.*

Gospel Acclamation

Ceiliúradh an tSoiscéil

Each section is sung by the choir and repeated by the congregation

Holy, Holy, Holy

Is naofa, naofa, naofa

Memorial Acclamation
Comhgháir tar éis an Choisreacain

Each section of the music is sung by the choir and repeated by all.

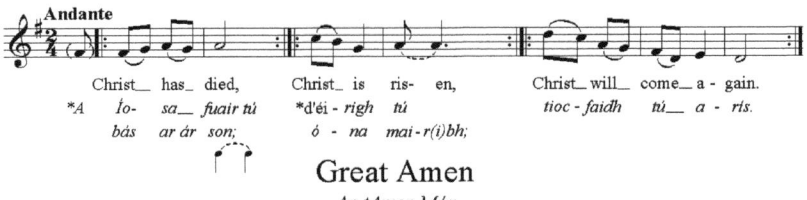

Great Amen
An tAmen Mór

Each section of the music is sung by the choir in unison and repeated by the congregation.

Our Father
Ár nAthair

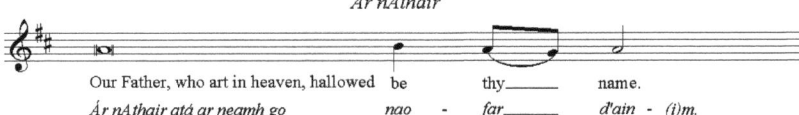

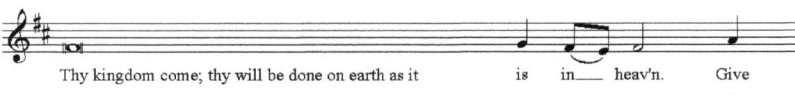

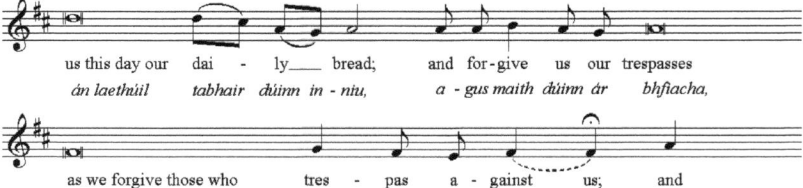

*For these two acclamations in Irish, the music needs to be sung twice in order to fit the words. This applies to both choir and congregation.

Lamb of God
A Uain Dé

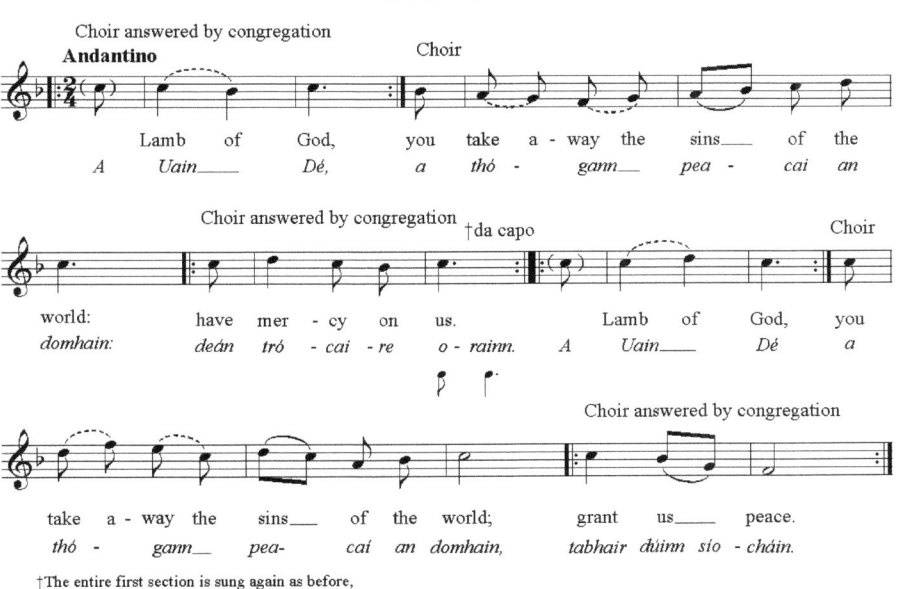

†The entire first section is sung again as before, complete with all answers by the congregation.

Appendix 1 | Seóirse Bodley's Sacred Music

Genre/Title	Musical Forces	Date Composed
Religious Cantatas		
A Concert Mass*	Soloists: Soprano, Mezzo	1984
Text by Seóirse Bodley	Soprano, Tenor and Bass, SATB	
1984	Choir, & String Orchestra.	
Fraw Musica*	Mezzo Soprano,	1996
Texts: Martin Luther	Mixed-voice Choir,	
& Johann Walter	String Orchestra,	
	Flute, Bassoon (Optional)	
	& Organ.	
Instrumental Works		
Salve Maria Virgo*	Orchestra	1957
Chiaroscuro*	Piano Solo	1999
(The Taking of Christ)		
Congregational Mass Settings		
Mass of Peace	Celebrant or Cantor	1976
	Choir (Unison/SATB)	
	Congregation & Organ	
Mass of Joy	Choir (Unison /SATB)	1978
	Congregation & Organ	
Mass of Glory	Choir (SSA or SSATBB)	1980
(Aifreann na Glóire)	Congregation, Organ	
	& Optional Instruments	
Psalm Settings		
Psalm 95	Cantor(s),	1979
('O Sing a new Song to the Lord')	Choir (SA or TB or SATB)	
	Congregation, Organ	
	& Optional Instruments	

* Available from the Contemporary Music Centre, Ireland. Email: info@cmc.ie
All other scores are available from the composer who can be contacted through the CMC.

The O Antiphons

'O Sapientia'
'O Adonai'
'O Radix Jesse'
'O Clavis David'
'O Oriens'
'O Rex Gentium'
'O Emmanuel'

Two or Three Cantors, Small Choir or Group, Congregation & Organ

1978
(Veritas, 1979)

Marian Hymns
'A Hymn to Our Lady' 1979
(Words: Michael Hodgetts)

Occasional Hymns
Hymn for the Congregation of St. Louis
(Words: Michael Hodgetts)

SSA or SATB or solo voice 1980

(with vocal (solo/group) or instrumental descant) Congregation, Organ or strings (Quartet or Orchestra)

Christmas Carols
Traditional German Carols

Title	Setting	Year
'Es sungen drei Engel'	Medium Voice & Piano	1997
'In dulci Jubilo'	Medium Voice & Piano	1997
'Maria durch ein' Dornwald ging'	Medium Voice & Piano	1997
'O komm, o komm, Emmanuel'	Medium Voice & Piano	1997

Traditional Irish Carols

Title	Setting	Year
'Dia do Bheatha a Mhic Mhuire'	Medium Voice & Piano	1995
'Don oíche úd i mBeitheal'	Medium Voice & Piano	1997
'In Bethlehem City'	Medium Voice & Piano/Harp	1988
Suantraí na Maighdine	Medium Voice & Harp/Piano	1988
'The Burning Babe'	Medium Voice & Harp	1988
'The Enniscorthy Christmas Carol'	Medium Voice & Piano	1985
'Upon my Lap my Sovereign Sits'	Medium Voice & Harp/Piano	1988

Text: Richard Rowlands

The Kilmore Carols

'A Carol for Christmas Day'	Medium Voice & Piano	1986
'A Carol for Twelfth Day'	Medium Voice & Piano (or Harpsichord or Harp) with Optional Parts for Cello and 2 Flutes	1986
'Song for Jerusalem'	Medium Voice & Piano	1986

Irish Religious Folksongs

A Athair Dhilis	Medium Voice & Piano	n.d.
An Spiorad Naomh Umainn	Medium Voice & Piano	n.d.
An tAiséirí'	Medium Voice & Piano	2001
An Teicheadh go hÉigipt	SSA	n.d.
Dán Molta Dé	Medium Voice & Harp	1988
Naomhtha Cearda Mhic Mhuire	Medium Voice & Piano	1995
Pósadh Naomhtha Cána	Medium Voice & Piano	1988

Traditional American Spiritual

Balm in Gilead	Medium Voice & Piano	2002

www.ingramcontent.com/pod-product-compliance
Ingram Content Group UK Ltd.
Pitfield, Milton Keynes, MK11 3LW, UK
UKHW021838210426
5322IPUK00021B/358